The Exploration of Interesting Websites on Internet

By Chung L. Pu

Introduction

The purpose of this paper is to illustrate that anyone with a computer can join me to explore and enjoy the Internet. I hasten to add that the computer must have a good audio output. This is because a large portion of the Internet covered in this paper deals with music.

The concept of Internet as we know today can be traced to early 1920s to Norbert Wiener, who was a Mathematics Professor at the Massachusetts Institute of Technology. It was known then as Cybernetics. It remained dormant until about 1950s to 1960s when computer became affordable to the general public.

I retired from the Charles Stark Draper Laboratory after 28 years as an engineer. The Laboratory pioneered the inertial guidance and control systems for aircraft and missiles. It was responsible for the guidance and control of the highly acclaimed Apollo Moon landing project.

My wife and I moved to Palo Alto, CA in August 2009. I became intrigued by the mystery of Internet. I acquired a iMac computer and began my journey into the exciting world of Internet. My venture began with a small number of arbitrarily chosen subjects of interest. Since then, the field of interest has been growing with no end in sight. Thus, a natural starting point is the Category of Interest.

(1)   Category of Interest

        1-1:   Apple
        1-2:   Yahoo
        1-3:   News - 1
        1-4:   News - 2
        1-5:   Talk show
        1-6:   Political news
        1-7:   Network news and magazine
        1-8:   Network morning news
        1-9:   Google
        1-10:   Sunday morning public affairs
        1-11:   Saturday night
        1-12:   Jeanette MacDonald and Nelson Eddy
        1-13:   George Gershwin
        1-14:   Music - 1
        1-15:   Music - 2
        1-16:   Popular sitcom
        1-17:   TV musical

1-18: Cartoon
1-19: Movie
1-20: Satire
1-21: Hulu
1-22: Magazine - 1
1-23: Magazine - 2
1-24: Piano
1-25: Waltz
1-26: Opera
1-27: Tchaikovsky
1-28: Lang Lang
1-29: Yo Yo Ma
1-30: Sarah Chang
1-31: Itzhak Perlman
1-32: Rachmaninoff
1-33: Weather
1-34: Boston Pops - 1
1-35: Boston Pops - 2
1-36: Boston Pops - 3
1-37: Boston Pops - 4
1-38: Boston Pops - 5
1-39: Operetta
1-40: Comedy act
1-41: Sport
1-42: Free online TV
1-43: Home box office
1-44: Rodgers and Hammerstein
1-45: Jerome Kern
1-46: Beethovan
1-47: Western
1-48: Lorentz Hart and Richard Rodgers
1-49: Andre Rieu
1-50: Marilyn Monroe
1-51: Sesame Street
1-52: Alfred Hitchcock
1-53: Charlie Chaplin
1-54: Anne Frank
1-55: The Godfather
1-56: Mitch Miller
1-57: Symphony
1-58: Barbra Streisand
1-59: Shirley Temple
1-60: Fred Astaire and Ginger Rogers
1-61: Elizabeth Taylor
1-62: Humphrey Bogart and Ingrid Bergman

1-63: Katharine Hepburn
1-64: Bette Davis
1-65: Joan Fontaine
1-66: Cole Porter
1-67: Bing Crosby
1-68: Clint Eastwood
1-69: Frank Sinatra
1-70: Perry Como
1-71: Jane Austen
1-72: Pride and Prejudice
1-73: Vladimir Horowitz
1-74: Jascha Heifetz
1-75: Arthur Rubinstein
1-76: Carol Channing
1-77: Julie Andrews
1-78: Broadway
1-79: Agatha Christie
1-80: Murder She Wrote
1-81: Matlock
1-82: Perry Mason
1-83: Pink Panther
1-84: Mission Impossible
1-85: Price Is Right
1-86: Wheel of Fortune
1-87: Sherlock Holmes
1-88: Radio City Rockettes
1-89: Jeanette MacDonald
1-90: Jane Fonda
1-91: Ingrid Bergman
1-92: Anthony Hopkins
1-93: The Graduate
1-94: Gone With The Wind
1-95: Caesar and Cleopatra
1-96: Who is Afraid of Virginia Woolf
1-97: Lassie
1-98: Lord of Rings
1-99: John Wayne
1-100: Dallas
1-101: Bridge on the River Kwai
1-102: Jeopardy
1-103: Who wants to be a millionaire
1-104: Dynasty
1-105: The French Connection
1-106: Wall Street
1-107: Shakespeare
1-108: The King and I

1-109: Midnight Cowboy
1-110: Lucille Ball
1-111: Wizard of Oz
1-112: Watch Friends Online
1-113: Keeping Up Appearances
1-114: The Beatles

The categories mentioned above are equivalent to Bookmarks in computer terminology. These Bookmarks are arranged in a row directly over each website for easy access. Simultaneously, a Bookmarks command is placed over the center of each website so that any member of a particular Bookmark may be activated or clicked.

(2)   Process of Compilation with iMac computer

2-1:   Click the Bookmarks and All Bookmarks.
2-2:   Enter the name of a website for a chosen Category, say "Music". Go to Google or Yahoo Search to search this website to be stored. Click to enter.
2-3:   Enter the name of the website to be stored. Click to enter. The chosen website will show up. Click the (+) sign on the address Bar. A panel will drop down asking for your confirmation to store this website in the category you have chosen in step 2-2, i.e.: "Music".
2-4:   Go back to Bookmarks and All Bookmarks. The name of your website in step 2-3 should be listed under "Music".
2-5:   You have now compiled your website to your chosen category.
2-6:   Repeat step 2-1 to step 2-5 for additional websites to be stored.

(3)   Components of subjects under Category of Interest

        1-1:   Apple
                Welcome to Apple Store (USA)

        1-2:   Yahoo
                Yahoo
                Yahoo Mail
                Yahoo News
                Yahoo Search
                Yahoo Maps

        1-3:   News - 1
                NBC Bay Area News
                CNN News
                CNN on Twitter
                The New York Times
                The Washington Post
                San Francisco Chronicle
                The Los Angeles Times
                San Jose Mercury News
                The Washington Times
                PBS News Hour
                The Wall Street Journal
                The Huffington Post
                The Week Magazine
                The Economist
                The Onion News Network
                Current TV
                BBC News
                US News and World Report
                NPR - National Public Radio
                CNBC
                MSNBC
                Technology News - CNET
                National Journal
                The Atlantic
                Financial Times - ft.com
                Bloomberg Businessweek
                The Guardian
                The Boston Globe
                Chicago Tribune
                Shanghai Daily
                You tube - Russia Today
                C-Span - Washington Journal
                Roll Call - Newspaper of Capitol

ABC Green Room
New York Observer

1-4:   News - 2

Qindao News (Qindao, China)
People's Daily Online - Home Page (China):
AJE - Al Jazeera English
The Sun
New York Daily News
Swiss News
China Daily - US Edition
South China Morning Post (Hong Kong)
Taipei Times
Der Spiegel
San Diego Union Tribune
Detroit Free Press
New York Post
USA Today
Oakland Tribune
Christian Science Monitor
The Daily News (Palo Alto, CA)
Palo Alto Online
San Mateo Daily Journal
The Daily Telegraph
The Times - UK
CBC News - Canada
London Times
The Atlanta Journal & Constitution Newspaper - AJC
San Francisco Examiner
The Nation
Philly.com
Bing News - Microsoft
Express.com - UK
Mail Online - UK
The Strait Times - Singapore
News of the World - UK
Chicago Sun Times
The Daily Mirror - UK
Deutsche Welle: DW-World.DE
You tube - Wall Street Journal Report with Maria Bartiromo
PBS - Nightly Business News

1-5:   Talk show
                The McLaughlin Group
                The Chris Matthews Show
                Hard Ball with Chris Matthews
                The Daily Beast
                Washington Week
                Charles Kruthammer Column
                Inside Washington
                The Daily Show with Jon Stewart
                The Colbert Report
                The Rachel Maddow Show
                Morning Joe
                The Last Word with Lawrence O'Donnell
                The View
                Dr. Oz
                Bill Moyers Journal
                Charlie Rose

1-6:   Political news
                Political News - Politiico.com
                The Cook Political Report
                American Enterprise Institute

1-7:   Network news and magazine
                NBC News
                ABC News
                CBS News
                FOX News
                Weekly Magazine 60 Minutes
                Discovery Channel
                History Channel
                Dish Network

1-8:   Network morning news
                Today - NBC
                Good Morning America - ABC
                The Early Show - CBS

1-9:   Google
                Google Search
                Google News
                Google Maps

1-10: Sunday morning public affairs
           Meet the Press -NBC
           This Week with Christiane Amanpour - ABC
           Face the Nation - CBS
           Sunday News with Chris Wallace - FOX

1-11: Saturday night
           Saturday Night Live

1-12: Jeanette MacDonald and Nelson Eddy
           You tube - Kiss from an angel
           You tube - Wanting you
           You tube - I'll see you
           You tube - Sweetheart
           You tube - Rose Marie
           You tube - Indian love song
           You tube - Indian love call
           You tube - Bitter Sweet

1-13: George Gershwin
           You tube - Summertime
           You tube - An American in Paris
           You tube - I got rhythm
           You tube - Rhapsody in Blue
           You tube - I love you Porgy
           You tube - Bess, you is my woman now

1-14: Music - 1
           You tube - Massenet: Meditation from Thais
           You tube - Ponchielle: Dance of the hours
           You tube - Offenbach: Barcarolle from Tales of Hoffmann
           You tube - Rimsky Korsakov: Scheherazade
           You tube - Ravel: Borelo
           You tube - Mascagni: Rusticana
           You tube - Schubert: Ave Maria
           You tube - Saint-Saens: Carnival of animals
           You tube - Beethovan: 5th Symphony 1st mvt
           You tube - Beethovan: 5th Symphony 2nd mvt
           You tube - Beethovan: 5th Symphony 3rd mvt
           You tube - Beethovan: 5th Symphony 4th mvt
           You tube - Weber (Toscanini) : Invitation to the dance
           You tube - The Call of the Wild: Dog of the Yukon
           You tube - Song of India from Opera Sadko (piano)
           You tube - Slim Whitman: Indian love song
           You tube - Jeanette MacDonald and Nelson Eddy:
                      Indian love call (from 1936 film Rose Marie)

You tube - Doris Day: On the sunny side of the street
You tube - Tommy Dorsey: Marie
You tube - Rose Marie (1954) part 1
You tube - Rachmaninov: Rhapsody from a theme by Paganini
You tube - Lawrence Welk Show: Song of India
You tube - Rimsky Korsakov: Song of India (Choice 603)

1-15: Music - 2

You tube - Borodin: String quartet No. 2
You tube - Borodin: Prince Igor
You tube - Rimsky Korsakov: Flight of bumble bee
You tube - Rimsky Korsakov: Song of India
You tube - Rimsky Korsakov: Dance of the tumbler
You tube - Rimsky Korsakov: Arabian Song
You tube - Rimsky Korsakov: A panorama of his best work
You tube - Rimsky Korsakov: Scheherazade
You tube - Rimsky Korsakov: Young prince and princess
You tube - Rimsky Korsakov: Younh prince and princess (violin)
You tube - Rimsky Korsakov: Capriccio Espagnol
You tube - Rimsky Korsakov: Russian Easter Festival Overture
You tube - Rimsky Korsakov: Indian love song (violin)
You tube - Bizet: L'Arlesienne Suite No. 1 Prelude
You tube - Marlinsky: Ballet Scheherazade part 1
You tube - Marlinsky: Ballet Scheherazade part 2
You tube - Dancing on string performs Song of India
You tube - Debussy: Clair de lune
You tube - Debussy: Reverie
You tube - Hoagy Carmichael: Star Dust
You tube - Stravinsky: The Rite of Spring
You tube - Stravinsky: Firebird
You tube - Dvorak: The New World Symphony
You tube - Symphony of Science: DNA and Life
You tube - Symphony of Science: Our place in the Comoos
You tube - Dr. Zhivago, Lara's theme
You tube - Lawrence Welk Show: Adios, Au Revoir, Aufweidersehn
You tube - Artie Shaw Concert for Clarinet
You tube - Duke Ellington Orchestra: Satin Doll
You tube - Benny Goodman: Sing Sing Sing
You tube - Horowitz: Chopin Sonata No. 2
You tube - Rubinstein: Brahms piano concerto No. 1
You tube - Susan Boyle: I dreamed a dream - original version
You tube - Susan Boyle on British Got Talent

1-16: Popular sitcom

        You tube - All in the family theme song 1971
        You tube - Maude's dilemma on "condom" skit
        You tube - Golden Girls
        You tube - Keeping up appearance
        You tube - Waiting for God
        You tube - Perry Mason
        You tube - Jerry Seinfeld
        You tube - Top 10 Seinfeld best moments
        You tube - Friends: Show tribute
        You tube - Friends: Ending
        You tube - Friends: Unseen clip
        You tube - Office: Office
        You tube - Office: TV show
        You tube - Mr. Bean: Ice Ballet
        You tube - Mr. Bean: Wedding
        You tube - Mr. Bean: Jail

1-17: TV musical

        You tube - Oklahoma
        You tube - My Fair Lady (1964) Trailer
        You tube - The Music Man "ya got trouble"
        You tube - Mary Poppins
        You tube - My Favorable Things
        You tube - Sound of Music
        You tube - Oh, what a beautiful morning, Oklahoma
        You tube - The Wizard of Oz
        You tube - My Fair Lady: The Rain in Spain
        You tube - I could dance all night
        You tube - My Fair Lady: The Embassy Ball
        You tube - My Fair Lady : Horse race scene

1-18: Cartoon

        New Yorker Magazine cartoon and comic
        You tube - Snow White and Seven Dwarfs
        The Week Magazine cartoon

1-19: Movie
              You tube - Gone with the wind (trailer)
              You tube - Judgement at Nurenberg
              You tube - Schindler's List: Main theme
              You tube - The Great Escape
              You tube - A Tale of Two Cities
              You tube - Charles Boyer: Gaslight
              You tube - Audrey Hepburn: Wait until Dark
              You tube - Audrey Hepburn: Breakfast at Tiffany's
              You tube - Audrey: Roman Holiday
              You tube - Witness for the Prosecution

1-20: Satire
              Political satire

1-21: Hulu
              Hulu - Movie Home
              Hulu - TV Home

1-22: Magazine - 1
              Slate Magazine
              The American Prospect
              Weekly Standard
              The New Yorker
              People Magazine
              Popular Mechanics
              Popular Science
              Consumer Report
              Vogue - Fashion
              Elle - Fashion
              New York Magazine
              The New Republic
              Sports Illustrated
              Rolling Stone

1-23: Magazine - 2
              National Review Online
              Salon.com
              Newsweek
              Time
              National Inquirer
              Forbes
              Esquire
              Fortune
              National Geographic Magazine

1-24: Piano

        You tube - Van Cliburn: Beethovan piano concerto No. 5
        You tube - Van Cliburn: Tchaikvsky piano concerto No. 1
        You tube - Van Cliburn: Debussy Clair de lune
        You tube - David Fung: Tchaikovsky piano concerto No. 1
              1st movement
        You tube - Argerich: Tchaikovsky piano concerto No. 1
              2nd movement
        You tube - Argerich: Tchaikovsky piano concerto No. 1
              3rd movement
        You tube - Chopin: Fantasie Impromptu, Op. 66
        You tube - Chopin: Military polonaise
        You tube - Chopin: Nocturne in E - flat
        You tube - Mozart: Rondo Alla Turca (Turkish march)
        You tube - Debussy: Clair de lune
        You tube - Debussy: Reverie
        You tube - Bizet: Prelude from L'Arlesienne Suite
        You tube - Schumann: Traumerei
        You tube - Song of India (piano)

1-25: Waltz

        You tube - Waldteufel: Espana Waltz
        You tube - Strauss: Overture to Die Fledermaus
        You tube - Strauss: Blue Danube
        You tube - Strauss: Roses from the south, Op. 388
        You tube - Strauss: Tales of Vienna woods, Op. 325
        You tube - Strauss: Emperor Waltz, Op. 437
        You tube - Strauss: Thunder & Lightening polka, Op. 324
        You tube - Strauss: Annen polka, Op. 117
        You tube - Strauss: Vienna blut, Op. 354
        You tube - Strauss: Artists life waltz

1-26: Opera

        You tube - Bizet: Carmen
        You tube - Puccini: Madam Butterfly
        You tube - Rossini: The Barber of Seville
        You tube - Verdi: La Traviata
        You tube - Offenbach: Orpheus in the underworld
        You tube - Von Suppe: Overture to the light Cavalry
        You tube - Mozart: The marriage of Figaro

1-27: Tchaikovsky
        You tube - Tchaikovsky 1812 Overture
        You tube - Romeo and Juliet
        You tube - Van Cliburn: Tchaikovsky piano concerto No. 1
                1st movemevnt
        You tube - Van Cliburn: Tchaikovsky piano concerto No. 1
                2nd movement
        You tube - Van Cliburn: Tchaikovsky piano concerto No. 1
                3rd movement
        You tube - Tchaikovsky: None but the lonely heart
        You tube - Tchaikovsky: Sleeping beauty waltz
        You tube - Tchaikovsky: Dance of the swans
        You tube - Tchaikovsky: The nutcracker snow flakes
        You tube - Van Cliburn wins First Tchaikovsky Competition

1-28: Lang Lang
        You tube - 2011 New Year Concert (1)
        You tube - Tchaikovsky piano concerto No. 1, 2nd mvt
        You tube - Tchaikovsky piano concerto No. 1, 3rd mvt
        You tube - Rachmaninov piano concerto No. 2, 1st mvt
        You tube - Rachmaninov piano concerto No. 2, 2nd mvt
        You tube - Liszt: Hungarian Rhapsody No. 2
        You tube - Liszt: Liebstraum

1-29: Yo Yo Ma
        You tube - Bach: Cello suite No. 1
        You tube - Paganini:Caprice 24 on cello
        You tube - Saint-Saens: Swan
        You tube - Massenet: Meditation from Thais

1-30: Sarah Chang
        You tube - Mendelssohn: Violin concerto mvt 1
        You tube - Tchaikovsky: Violin concerto part 1
        You tube - Vivaldi: The Four Seasons
        You tube - Paganini: Cantabile
        You tube - Massenet: Meditation from Thais

1-31: Itzhak Perlman
        You tube - Mendelssohn violin concerto
        You tube - Vivaldi: The Four Seasons, Spring
        You tube - Mozart: Rondo for violin and orchestra
        You tube - Stravinsky: Suite part a I-III (1.2)
        You tube - Chopin: Nocturne in C# minor

1-32: Rachmaninov
> You tube - Plays his piano concerto No. 2, 1st mvt
> You tube - Rachmaninov piano concerto No. 2, 1st mvt
> You tube - Rachmaninov piano concerto No. 2, 2nd mvt
> You tube - Rachmaninov piano concerto No. 2 , 3rd mvt
> You tube - Rachmaninov plays Rhapsody on a theme by
> Paganini

1-33: Weather
> The Weather Channel
> Accu Weather

1-34: Boston Pops - 1
> You tube - The Stars and Stripes Forever
> You tube - Copland: An Outdoor Overture
> You tube - Bernstein: Candide Overture music from "Mass"
> You tube - Wilson: 7 Trombone (The Music Man)
> You tube - Gershwin: Three Preludes
> You tube - Crazy For You
> You tube - Anderson: Forgotten Dreams
> You tube - Anderson: A Trumpeter's Lullaby
> You tube - Anderson: Bugler's Holiday
> You tube - Carmichael: Stardust
> You tube - Harline: When you wish upon a star
> You tube - Joplin: The Entertainer
> You tube - Joplin: Sugar Cane Rag
> You tube - Joplin: The Easy Winner
> You tube - Joplin: Maple Leaf Rag
> You tube - Blake: Charleston Rag
> You tube - Berlin: Alexander's Ragtime Band
> You tube - Bowman: 12th Street Rag
> You tube - Louis Armstrong: Tiger Rag
> You tube - Brook: Your will
> You tube - Shostakovich: Festive Overture
> You tube - Mendelssohn: Wedding March from a
> Midnight Dream
> You tube - Bach: Toccato and Figue in D minor

1-35: Boston Pops - 2
> You tube - Bach: Fugue a la Gique
> You tube - Bach: Sinfonia from Easter
> You tube - Bach: Violin solo Partita No. 3
> You tube - Bach: Sheep may safely graze
> You tube - Vaughan Williams: English folk song suite
> You tube - Tchaikovsky: 1812 Overture
> You tube - Sullivan: Overture di Ballo
> You tube - Ravel: Borelo

You tube - Verdi: Ballet music from Aida
You tube - Dvorak: Slavonic dance
You tube - Mussorgsky: Night on a Bald Mountain
You tube - Saint-Saens: Dance Macabre
You tube - Stravinsky: Infernal dance from Firebird
You tube - Ginastere: Estania - Danza final (Malambo)
You tube - Rembrandt & Strauss: The Gypsy Baron
You tube - Strauss: Tales from the Vienna Woods (waltz)
You tube - Strauss: Perpetual Motion Found
You tube - Strauss: Tritsch - Tratsch Polka

1-36: Boston Pops - 3
You tube - Strauss: Chinese Galop
You tube - Bach: Jeus, Joy of Man's Desiring
You tube - Goldmark: "Friemds Overture"
You tube - Debussy: Clair de lune
You tube - Sibelius: Finlandia
You tube - Grieg: In the hall of the Mountain King
You tube - Tchaikovsky: Dance of the reed flutes
You tube - Humperdinck: Hansel and Gretel
You tube - Dukas: The Sorcerer's Apprentice
You tube - Klensinger: Tubby the tuba
You tube - Dood: Mickey Mouse March
You tube - Churchill: Snow White and the Seven Dwarf
          Fantasy
You tube - Raposo: Sesame Street Theme
You tube - Melanie: Salka Brand New Key
You tube - Nichols: We've Only Just Begin
You tube - MacDermot: Aquarius
You tube - Gade: Jalousie
You tube - Artie Shaw: Star Dust

1-37: Boston Pops - 4
You tube - Schmidt: Can't Help Falling in Love
You tube - Frank Sinatra: September song
You tube - Porter: Night and Day
You tube - Shirley Jones: It might as well be Spring
You tube - Shermann: Medley from Mary Poppins
You tube - Bock: Medley from Fiddler in the Roof
You tube - Leigh: Medley from Man of La Mancha
You tube - Sondheim: Medley from Company
You tube - MacDermot: Medley from Hair
You tube - Barry: Midnight Cowboy

You tube - Bacharach: Rain drops keep falling on my head
You tube - Legrand: Summer of '42
You tube - Legrand: The Summer knows
You tube - Brooks: Micol's theme
You tube - Karin: From all we know
You tube - Rota: Love theme from the Godfather
You tube - Andre Rieu: Love theme from Romeo and Juliet
You tube - Mancini: Days of wine and roses
You tube - Barbra Streisand: Send me the clown
You tube - Mancini: Robinhood theme
You tube - John Williams: Theme from Jaws and Star War

1-38:   Boston Pops - 5
You tube - John Williams: Star War medley
You tube - John Williams: Jurassic Park
You tube - John Williams: Indiana Jones
You tube - Henry Mancini: Moon River
You tube - Henry Mancini: Breakfast at Tiffany's
You tube - Henry Mancini: Dr, Zhivago
You tube - Henry Mancini: As time goes by (Casablanca)
You tube - Henry Mancini: Stardust
You tube - Henry Mancini: The Godfather

1-39:   Operetta
You tube - Sigmund Romberg: Overture to Student Prince
You tube - Sigmund Romberg: Love comes back to me
You tube - Sigmund Romberg: Blossom
You tube - Victor Herbert: Naughty Marietta
You tube - Victor Herbert: When you are away
You tube - Gilbert Sullivan: The Mikado
You tube - Gilbert Sullivan: H.M.S. Pinafore
You tube - Rodolf Firmi: Chanson "in love"
You tube - Bernstein: Candide

1-40:   Comedy act
You tube - Comedy Central
You tube - Bill Maher
You tube - 30 Rock
Tbs.com - Conan O'Brien
You tube - Snooki
You tube - El Loco
You tube - Max and Peter
You tube - Jay Stewart & Mike Smith - The Egg Show
You tube - Just Clown Larry on Family Feud
You tube - Jackie Gleason
You tube - Bob Hope

You tube - Jack Benny
You tube - Red Skelton

1-41: Sport
Golf Channel
ESPN
Tennis Channel
NBA.com
MLB.com
NFL.com
NHL.com

1-42: Free online TV
Al Jazeera TV Channel

1-43: Home box office (HBO)
Comedy

1-44: Rodgers and Hammerstein
You tube - If I love you - Carousal
You tube - South Pacific
You tube - The King and I
You tube - State Fair
You tube - Oklahoma
You tube - At the movies

1-45: Jerome Kern
You tube - Yesterday
You tube - Show Boat
You tube - Smoke gets in your eyes
You tube - Long ago and far away
You tube - All things we are
You tube - Faithfully by journey
You tube - I have nothing

1-46: Beethovan
You tube - Moonlight Sonata
You tube - Fur Elise
You tube - Symphony No. 5
You tube - String quartet No. 4

1-47: Western
You tube - Gunsmoke part 1
You tube - Gunsmoke part 2
You tube - Gunsmoke part 3
You tube - Gunsmoke part 4

You tube - Gunsmoke part 5

1-48: Lorentz Hart and Richard Rodgers
You tube - Blue Moon
You tube -The Lady is a Tramp

1-49: Andre Rieu
You tube - Shostakovich Second Waltz
You tube - Theme from Romeo and Juliet
You tube - Vienna, city of my dream
You tube - Hava Nagila
You tube - The Blue Danube
You tube - Don't cry for me, New York City

1-50: Marilyn Monroe
You tube - Seven Year Itch
You tube - Some Like It Hot
You tube - Diamonds are Girls Best Friend
You tube - Bye Bye Baby
You tube - My Heart Belongs to Daddy

1-51: Sesame Street
You tube - Ernie and his rubber ducky
You tube - Elmo's song
You tube - S is for Song
You tube - Cookie Monster makes a sandwich

1-52: Alfred Hitchcock
You tube - Rear Window
You tube - The Birds
You tube - Nortorious part 1
You tube - Nortorious part 2
You tube - Nortorious part 3
You tube - Psycho

1-53: Charlie Chaplin
You tube - The lion's cage
You tube - The circus
You tube - Final speech in The Great Dictator
You tube - A beautiful Sunday morning
You tube - Charlie Chaplin

1-54: Anne Frank
        You tube - The Whole Story Part 1
        You tube - The Whole Story Part 2
        You tube - The Whole Story Part 3
        You tube - The Whole Story Part 4

1-55: The Godfather
        You tube - Al Pacino: The Sound Track
        You tube - The theme song
        You tube - Marlon Brando: don corleone
        You tube - Music video

1-56: Mitch Miller
        You tube - Sing Along with Mitch (1 of 4)
        You tube - Sing Along with Mitch (2 of 4)
        You tube - Sing Along with Mitch (3 of 4)
        You tube - Sing Along with Mitch (4 of 4)

1-57: Symphony
        You tube - Beethovan: Symphony No. 5
        You tube - Beethovan: Symphony No. 9
        You tube - Boston Symphony: Brahm's Symphony No. 4
        You tube - Boston Symphony: Mahler's Symphony No. 2

1-58: Barbra Streisand
        You tube - The way we were
        You tube - Cry me a river
        You tube - Lover, come back to me
        You tube - Send me the clown

1-59: Shirley Temple
        You tube - Bright Eyes
        You tube - Little Miss Broadway
        You tube - Curly Top

1-60: Fred Astaire and Ginger Rogers
        You tube - Love you madly
        You tube - Come on and dance
        You tube - I won't dance
        You tube - Lets' face the music and dance

1-61: Elizabeth Taylor
        You tube - Dame Elizabeth Taylor: Attribute
        You tube - A video tribute
        You tube - Movie Legends - Elizabeth Taylor (Finale)
        You tube - Things of Beauty

1-62: Humphrey Bogart and Ingrid Bergman
    You tube - Casablanca - As time goes by
    You tube - Play it again Sam
    You tube - Casablanca Final
    You tube - Scene fro Casablanca movie

1-63: Katharine Hepburn
    You tube - Philadelphia Story
    You tube - Guess who's coming for dinner
    You tube - Her only Academy Award Appearance
    You tube - Oscar and portraits at National Portrait Gallery

1-64: Bette Davis
    You tube - Tribute to "Jezebel"
    You tube - What a Dump
    You tube - The Little Foxes
    You tube - Bitches about ingratitude

1-65: Joan Fontaine
    You tube - Screen test for Rebecca (1940)
    You tube - Serinade (1940)
    You tube - Suspicion part 1 (1940)
    You tube - Suspicion part 2 (1941)
    You tube - Suspicion part 3 (1941)
    You tube - Suspicion part 4 (1941)

1-66: Cole Porter
    You tube - Anything Goes
    You tube - Begin The Beguine
    You tube - Day and Night
    You tube - You're The Top

1-67: Bing Crosby
    You tube - White Christmas
    You tube - Silent Night
    You tube - Rudolph The Red Nosed Reindeer
    You tube - Young At Heart
    You tube - I Love Paris
    You tube - Mona Lisa
    You tube - Tea For Two
    You tube - My Blue Heaven
    You tube - September Song
    You tube - The Summer Wind
    You tube - It's Been a Long, Long Time
    You tube - "Swinging on a Star"
    You tube - Moonlight Becomes You

1-68: Clint Eastwood
        You tube - Dirty Harry (1971)
        You tube - Dirty Harry: The Enforcer
        You tube - Dirty Harry: Magnum Force
        You tube - Dirty Harry Interview Inspector Moore
        You tube - Dirty Harry: Bus Hijack

1-69: Frank Sinatra
        You tube - September Song (with lyric)
        You tube - That's Life
        You tube - Come Fly with Me
        You tube - New York, New York
        You tube - Its Always You

1-70: Perry Como
        You tube - Yesterday I heard The Rain
        You tube - I think of You
        You tube - And I Love You SoYou tube - If I Am Lucky
        You tube - The Wind Beneath My Wings
        You tube - I'm Always Chasing Rainbows
        You tube - If I Am Lucky

1-71: Jane Austen
        You tube - Becoming Jane Austen
        You tube - Be Mine Tonight
        You tube - Bleeding Love
        You tube - Kiss me Jane Austen Style

1-72: Pride and Prejudice
        You tube - Ordinary Day
        You tube - Official music video "From The Sea"
        You tube - Rain
        You tube - Main Theme
        You tube - "Have You Ever Been In Love"
        You tube - I Loved Her First
        You tube - I'm Your Angel
        You tube - Somewhere Only We Know
        You tube - Hanging By A Moment
        You tube - Stolen
        You tube - Sweet Surrender
        You tube - I'm Your Angel
        You tube - Blush (Only You)
        You tube - You and Me
        You tube - Listen to Your Heart
        You tube - Book of Love
        You tube - Every Time We Touch

1-73: Vladimir Horowitz

           You tube - Mozart: Piano concerto 23, 1st mvt
           You tube - Mozart: Piano concerto 23, 2nd mvt
           You tube - Mozart: Piano concerto 23, 3rd mvt
           You tube - Mozart: Sonata in C major, 1st mvt
           You tube - Beethovan: Piano concerto No. 5
           You tube - Chopin: Ballad
           You tube - Tchaikovsky: Piano concerto No. 1, 1st mvt
           You tube - Tchaikovsky: Piano concerto No. 1, 2nd mvt
           You tube - Tchaikovsky: Piano concerto No. 1, 3rd mvt
           You tube - Carmen: Fantasie
           You tube - Schumann: Toccata, Op. 7
           You tube - Liszt: Consolation No, 3
           You tube - Liszt/Schubert: Valse
           You tube - Beethovan:Moonlight Sonata, 1st mvt
           You tube - Scarlatti: Sonata L224
           You tube - Chopin: Piano Sonata No. 2
           You tube - Chopin: Polonaise, Op. 33 in A flat major

1-74: Jascha Heifetz

           You tube - Paganini: Caprice No. 24
           You tube - Mozart:Rondo
           You tube - Bach: Chaconne
           You tube - Tchaikovsky: Violin concerto, 1st mvt
           You tube - Tchaikovsky: Serenade Melancolique
           You tube - Brahms: Hungarian Dance No.7
           You tube - Prokofier: March
           You tube - Hora Staccato
           You tube - Gluck: Melodie
           You tube - Heifetz: Sweet Remembrance
           You tube - Heifetz: "When you make love"
           You tube - Bruch Scottish Fantasy - 2 (Allegro)
           You tube - Waxman - Carmen Fantasy
           You tube - Zigeunerweisen
           You tube - Heifetz pays Debussy
           You tube - Heifetz plays Ave Maria
           You tube - Heifetz plays Meditation

1-75: Arthur Rubinstein
      You tube - Brahms: Piano concerto No. 1
      You tube - Rubinstein plays Chopin (1950)
      You tube - Grieg piano concerto 1st mvt
      You tube - Grieg piano concerto 2nd mvt
      You tube - Grieg piano concerto 3rd mvt
      You tube - Rubinstein plays Rachmaninov
      You tube - Beethovan concerto No. 3, 1st mvt
      You tube - Beethovan Moonlight Sonata , 3rd mvt
      You tube - Chopin: Waltz No. 2, i n A minor
      You tube - Chopin: piano sonata No. 2
      You tube - De Falla's "Ritual Fire Dance"
      You tube - "La Campanella"
      You tube - Liszt: Hungarian Rhapsody No, 12
      You tube - Brahms concerto No. 2 in B flat
      You tube - Brahms piano concerto No. 2
      You tube - Rachmaninoff: Rhapsody on a theme by
              Paganini

1-76: Carol Channing
      You tube - "Diamonds Are a Girl's Best Friend"
      You tube - Jazz Baby
      You tube - Little Girl from Little Rock
      You tube - As Marlene Dietrich " Falling in Love Again"
      You tube - As Carmen Miranda
      You tube - As Cecilla Cission, silent film star
      You tube - Talk about "The Vamp" on Tonys
      You tube - On "Profile": Impressionist
      You tube - The Audition
      You tube - Sophie Tucker
      You tube - T. Bankhead

1-77: Julie Andrews
      You tube - The Von Trapp Children
      You tube - Sound of Music - 40th Reunion
      You tube - Sound of Musci- 40 years later
      You tube - The Real Marie Von Trapp
      You tube - The Von Trapp Family Singers
      You tube - Trapp Family sings Bach
      You tube - Sound of Music
      You tube - The Hills are Alive - The Sound of Music
      You tube - The Sound of Julie Andrews
      You tube - Julie Andrews on 60 minutes
      You tube - Julie Andrews - Victor/Victoria

1-78: Broadway

        You tube - A Chorus Line - (Finale)
        You tube - Cats Musical - Memory
        You tube - Jesus Superstar - Superstar
        You tube - Hair - Aquarius
        You tube - Lady Gaga - Bad Romance
        You tube - Broadway Baby by Bernadette Peters
        You tube - Shirley Bassy - Diamonds are Forever
        You tube - "America" - Westside Story
        You tube - The Phantom of the Opera
        You tube - Annie
        You tube - James Bond 007 (Tomorrow Never Dies)
        You tube - Madonna - Die Another Day
        You tube - Britney Spears - Toxic
        You tube - Baby its your Broadway Channel
        You tube - Wicked Broadway Show Feature
        You tube - Ragtime - The Musical Broadway Shoe Feature
        You tube - A Little Night Music Broadway Show Feature
        You tube - South Pacific Broadway Show Feature
        You tube - Bye Bye Birdie Broadway Show Feature
        You tube - Hair The Musical Broadway Show Feature
        You tube - Rock of the age - 0;5/25/09

1-79: Agatha Christie

        You tube - Agatha Christie
        You tube - Agatha Christie, An Autobiography
        You tube - Agatha's Poirot (Short Tribute)
        You tube - Poirot and the depth of Mrs. McGinty
        You tube - Poirot: One, Two, Buckle my shoe
        You tube - Agatha Christie's Miss Marplke -trailer
        You tube - Hercule Poirot - Cup of Coffee
        You tube - Poirot: Halloween party
        You tube - Poirot: A wage of murder
        You tube - Poirot: The ABC of murder
        You tube - Poirot: The mystery of hunter's lodge
        You tube - Poirot: The Cornish mystery
        You tube - Poirot: The Adventure of the Wester Star
        You tube - Poirot: The Adventure of the Egyptian Tombe
        You tube - Poirot: The Underdog
        You tube - Poirot: The jewel robbery at the Grand Metro
        You tube - Poirot: The Plymouth Express
        You tube - Poirot: The affair at the Victory Ball
        You tube - Poirot: The Super Seuth

1-80: Murder She Wrote
          You tube - Murder She Wrote
          You tube - Opening theme
          You tube - 1984 TV Promo
          You tube - That crazy JB Fletcher
          You tube - Curse of the Daanav
          You tube - The Celtic riddle
          You tube - Parker Stevenson
          You tube - Leann Callahan
          You tube - Gordon Thomson
          You tube - Jonathan Brandis
          You tube - Roscoe Born
          You tube - Vincent Irizarry
          You tube - Deidre Hall
          You tube - The ski lodge episode
          You tube - Wayne Rogers
          You tube - Dean Stockwell
          You tube - Kathryn Grayson
          You tube - Megan Mullally
          You tube - Kristy McNichol

1-81: Matlock
          You tube - Matlock Theme
          You tube - The Assault
          You tube - Hip Hop
          You tube - The Parents
          You tube - The D.A.
          You tube - The Clown
          You tube - The Prisoner
          You tube - The Godfather
          You tube - The Jury
          You tube - The Witness
          You tube - The Brothers
          You tube - The Buddies
          You tube - The Trial
          You tube - The Picture
          You tube - The Suspect
          You tube - The Hunting Party
          You tube - The Secret
          You tube - The Con Man
          You tube - The Victim
          You tube - The Evening News
          You tube - Nowhere To Turn
          You tube - The Abduction
          You tube - The Informer
          You tube - The Game Show

1-82: Perry Mason
        You tube - Perry Mason Opening Theme
        You tube - Perry Mason returns
        You tube - The Case of Killer Kiss
        You tube - Della Street Perry Mason Love me tender
        You tube - Della and Perry - A Deep Love
        You tube - Perry Proposes
        You tube - Perry and Della - I will
        You tube - Perry and Della kiss, mpg
        You tube - All do - Perry and Della
        You tube - Case of Constant Doyle
        You tube - Case of Drowning Duck
        You tube - Case of Coupon Man
        You tube - Case of Wicked Wives
        You tube - Case of the Twice Told Twist
        You tube - Case of the Watery Witness
        You tube - Case of the Spurious Sister
        You tube - Case of the Lucky Legs
        You tube - TV theme Park Avenue Beat
        You tube - Perry Mason rare 1966 color presentation
        You tube - Perry Mason - Ken Malansky
        You tube - Raymond Burr Tribute

1-83: Pink Panther
        You tube - Pink Panther theme song
        You tube - Pink Panther TV show theme song
        You tube - The all new Pink Panther show credit
        You tube - Pink Panther dance

1-84: Mission Impossible
        You tube - Mission Impossible theme song
        You tube - Mission Impossible 2 music video
        You tube - Mission Impossible TV show theme song
        You tube - Mission Impossible opening titles

1-85: Price is right
        You tube - Price is right first show opening
        You tube - Price is right - Wedding proposal
        You tube - Price is right Bob Barker's final show
        You tube - Drew Carey's Price is right premier episode intro

1-86: Wheel of Fortune
> You tube - Pat Sajak kisses Vanna White
> You tube - Pat Sajak and Vanna White Interview
> You tube - How Pat and Vanna got their jobs
> You tube - Pat and Vanna sing

1-87: Sherlock Holmes
> You tube - Sherlock Holmes mood swing
> You tube - Sherlock Holmes goes crazy
> You tube - Sherlock Holmes and the rose
> You tube - Sherlock Holmes too much cocaine again
> You tube - Sherlock Holmes safety dance
> You tube - Doctor Watson is funny

1-88: Radio City Rockettes
> You tube - The Rockettes at Rockefeller Plaza
> You tube - The Rockettes at Macy's Parade 2010
> You tube - The Rockettes with Susan Boyle at 2010
>   Christmas
> You tube - The Rockettes dances of the wooden soldiers

1-89: Jeanette MacDonald
> You tube - San Francisco
> You tube - La Traviata
> You tube - Jerusalem
> You tube - Love Me Tonight
> You tube -The Incomparable Jeanette MacDonald

1-90: Jane Fonda
> You tube - Winning an Oscar for "Klute"
> You tube - Excessive Machine from Barbarella
> You tube - Georgia Rule
> You tube - Jane Fonda Attribute

1-91: Ingrid Bergman
> You tube - Winning an Oscar for "Gaslight"
> You tube - Scenes from Notorious
> You tube - The Yellow Rolls-Royce
> You tube - A Walk in the Spring Rain
> You tube - Intermezzo: A Love Story

1-92: Anthony Hopkins

        You tube - The Silence of Lambs ("Rube") Monologue
        You tube - Anthony Hopkins Tribute
        You tube - Anthony "Hannibal" Hopkins answering machine
        You tube - Anthony Hopkins: Lecter and Me

1-93: The Graduate

        You tube - The Graduate (1967)
        You tube - The Graduate Graduates - Part 1
        You tube - The Graduate Graduates - Part 2
        You tube - The Graduate Graduates - Part 3
        You tube - The Graduate Graduates - Part 4
        You tube - Anne Bancroft in the 'Graduate' (1967)
        You tube - The Graduate Montage

1-94: Gone with the Wind

        You tube - Gone with the Wind
        You tube - Vivien Leigh as Scarlett O'Hara
        You tube - Vivien Leigh accepts her Oscar
        You tube - Rhett Butler and Scarlett O'Hara
        You tube - Civil War Talk
        You tube - Home to Tara
        You tube - I just Wanna Make Love To You
        You tube - It Ain't Over Till It's Over
        You tube - The End

1-95: Caesar and Cleopatra

        You tube - Caesar and Cleopatra 1945
        You tube - George Bernard Shaw
        You tube - Antony and Cleopatra
        You tube - The Deaths of Antony and Cleopatra
        You tube - Antony and Cleopatra meet in Rome

1-96: Who is Afraid of Virginia Woolf

        You tube - Arriving Home
        You tube - Get the Guests
        You tube - Pour me a drink
        You tube - Houseboy
        You tube - Final fight
        You tube - Total War

1-97: Lassie
        You tube - Lassie opening theme
        You tube - Lassie and Timmy
        You tube - Lassie theme
        You tube - Lassie comes home
        You tube - The Magic of Lassie, part 1
        You tube - The Magic of Lassie, part 2

1-98: Lord of Rings
        You tube - Voiceover
        You tube - The Two Towers (trailer)
        You tube - Rohan Army
        You tube - The Battles
        You tube - The Last Alliance

1-99: John Wayne
        You tube - El Dorado
        You tube - True Grit
        You tube - The Duke
        You tube - The Cowboys
        You tube - The Pledge of Allegiance

1-100: Dallas
        You tube - Dallas Theme Song
        You tube - The Complete Intro
        You tube - Family Ties
        You tube - Little House on the Prairie
        You tube -Final Episode (Spring 1991)

1-101: Bridge on the River Kwai
        You tube - Bridge on the River Kwai theme
        You tube - The River Kwai Colonel Bogey
        You tube - UK Military March Colonel Bogey
        You tube - Michael Cine sings Colonel Bogey March

1-102: Jeopardy
        You tube - Jeopardy theme song
        You tube - Think music
        You tube - Playing Jeopardy theme song on piano
        You tube - Playing Jeopardy theme song on flute
        You tube - Jeopardy on Steel Drums

1-103: Who wants to be a millionaire
> You tube - First question wrong
> You tube - Flirt Fail
> You tube - Major Fraud
> You tube - Stupid Woman
> You tube - Huge Idiot

1-104: Dynasty
> You tube - Dynasty Theme Music (Season 1)
> You tube - Dynasty Season 1 Credits
> You tube - Dynasty Season 2 Opening Credits
> You tube - Dynasty Tribute - Best soap opera ever
> You tube - Memories from Dynasty Reunion

1-105: The French Connection
> You tube - The French Connection
> You tube - Gene Hackman winning an Oscar for it
> You tube - The French Connection - Video Tribute
> You tube - The Toughest Cop on the Block
> You tube - Best car chase ever

1-106: Wall Street
> You tube - "Gordon Gekko" is back, Money never sleep
> You tube - Gordon Gekko - "I create nothing, I own."
> You tube - Gordon Gekko: Greed is good
> You tube - Wall Street - Gordon Gekko
> You tube - Gordon Gekko's Greatest Hits(Wall Street 1987)

1-107: Shakespeare
> You tube - King Lear - Sir Laurence Olivier
> You tube - Hamlet - To Be Or Not To be - Laurence Olivier
> You tube - Macbeth
> You tube - A Midsummer Night Dream

1-108: The King and I
> You tube - Getting to Know You
> You tube - Shall We Dance
> You tube - Deborah Kerr receiving an Honorary Oscar
> You tube - Deborah Kerr and Yul Brynner

1-109: Midnight Cowboy
> You tube - Midnight Cowboy movie 1969 best film
> You tube - Midnight Cowboy Tribute - Solitary Man
> You tube - Midnight Cowboy - The sound of silence
> You tube - Midnight Cowboy Ending, Final Scene

1-110:   Lucille Ball
         You tube - Lucille Ball 100th Birthday Celebration
         You tube - Here's Lucy Promo
         You tube - Lucy's Big Break
         You tube - The Best of I Love Lucy

1-111:   Wizard of Oz
         You tube - The Enchanted movie planned
         You tube - Sam Raimi in talk to direct the movie
         You tube - Return to Oz Review by Siskel and Ebert
         You tube - Dorothy's Silver Slippers

1-112:   Watch Friends Online
         You tube - Watch Friends Episodes Online
         You tube - Friends - Revealing Secrets
         You tube - The best of Joey
         You tube - Rachel is having a baby
         You tube - Phoebe's best scenes
         You tube - Ross loves Friends
         You tube - Best of Chandler
         You tube - Monica obsessive compulsive
         You tube - Cast of Friends presenting an Emmy Award

         To watch old episodes, see website: iwatchfriends.com

1-113:   Keeping Up Appearances
         You tube - Golfing With The Major
         You tube - Onslows Birthday
         You tube - Singing For Emmett
         You tube - A Picnic For Daddy
         You tube - Elizabeth Spills The Coffee
         You tube - Rose has a new Christian boyfriend

1-114:   The Beatles
         You tube - Here Comes The Sun
         You tube - Blackbird
         You tube - All You Need Is Love
         You tube - Don't Let Me Down
         You tube - I Wanna Be Your Man